People in My Community

Librarian

by Jacqueline Laks Gorman
Photographs by Gregg Andersen

Reading consultant: Susan Nations, M.Ed., author/literacy coach/consultant

Please visit our web site at: **www.earlyliteracy.cc**
For a free color catalog describing Weekly Reader® Early Learning Library's
list of high-quality books, call 1-877-445-5824 (USA) or 1-800-387-3178 (Canada).
Weekly Reader® Early Learning Library's fax: (414) 336-0164.

Library of Congress Cataloging-in-Publication Data

Gorman, Jacqueline Laks, 1955-
    Librarian / by Jacqueline Laks Gorman.
      p. cm. — (People in my community)
    Summary: A simple introduction to the work of librarians in a library.
    Includes bibliographical references and index.
    ISBN 0-8368-3296-5 (lib. bdg.)
    ISBN 0-8368-3303-1 (softcover)
    1. Librarians—Juvenile literature. 2. Libraries—Juvenile literature.
  [1. Librarians. 2. Occupations. 3. Libraries.] I. Title.
    Z682.G68   2002
    020'.23—dc21   2002024199

This edition first published in 2002 by
Weekly Reader® Early Learning Library
330 West Olive Street, Suite 100
Milwaukee, WI 53212 USA

Copyright © 2002 by Weekly Reader® Early Learning Library

Art direction and page layout: Tammy Gruenewald
Photographer: Gregg Andersen
Editorial assistant: Diane Laska-Swanke
Production: Susan Ashley

Printed in the United States of America

1 2 3 4 5 6 7 8 9 06 05 04 03 02

Note to Educators and Parents

Reading is such an exciting adventure for young children! They are beginning to integrate their oral language skills with written language. To encourage children along the path to early literacy, books must be colorful, engaging, and interesting; they should invite the young reader to explore both the print and the pictures.

People in My Community is a new series designed to help children read about the world around them. In each book young readers will learn interesting facts about some familiar community helpers.

Each book is specially designed to support the young reader in the reading process. The familiar topics are appealing to young children and invite them to read — and re-read — again and again. The full-color photographs and enhanced text further support the student during the reading process.

In addition to serving as wonderful picture books in schools, libraries, homes, and other places where children learn to love reading, these books are specifically intended to be read within an instructional guided reading group. This small group setting allows beginning readers to work with a fluent adult model as they make meaning from the text. After children develop fluency with the text and content, the book can be read independently. Children and adults alike will find these books supportive, engaging, and fun!

— Susan Nations, M.Ed., author, literacy coach,
and consultant in literacy development

The librarian has an important job. The librarian helps people.

The librarian
works in the
library. The
librarian works
with books.

The librarian knows a lot about books. She decides what books to buy for the library.

The librarian puts the books on the **shelves**. Each book has to go in the right place.

shelves

When you visit
the library, the
librarian helps
you. She answers
all your questions.

Do you know what book you want? The librarian can help you find it.

Do you want to take a book home? The librarian can help you get a **library card**.

library card

The librarian checks out all your books and tells you when to bring them back.

It looks like fun
to be a librarian.
Would you like to
be a librarian
some day?

Glossary

librarian — a person who works in a library

library — a place where people can use or borrow magazines, books, videos, and other things

library card — a special card that is used by someone to check things out of a library

shelves — thin pieces of wood or metal that hold books

For More Information

Fiction Books

Deedy, Carmen Agra. *The Library Dragon*. Atlanta: Peachtree, 1994.

Williams, Suzanne. *Library Lil*. New York: Dial, 1997.

Nonfiction Books

Flanagan, Alice K. *Ms. Davison, Our Librarian*. New York: Children's Press, 1997.

Kottke, Jan. *A Day with a Librarian*. New York: Children's Press, 2000.

Web Sites

What Does a Librarian Do?

www.whatdotheydo.com/libraria.htm

For information on a librarian's job

KidsConnect

www.ala.org/ICONN/AskKC.html

Send an email question to a real librarian, and get an answer back

Index

About the Author

Jacqueline Laks Gorman is a writer and editor. She grew up in New York City and began her career working on encyclopedias and other reference books. Since then, she has worked on many different kinds of books. She lives with her husband and children, Colin and Caitlin, in DeKalb, Illinois.